KID CHEFS

COOKING WITH VEGGIES

Rose Miles

Enslow PUBLISHING

Please visit our website, www.enslow.com. For a free color catalog of all our high-quality books,
call toll free 1-800-398-2504 or fax 1-877-980-4454

Published in 2027 by
Enslow Publishing
2544 Clinton Street
Buffalo, NY 14224

Portions of this work were originally authored by Kristen Rajczak and published as I*ngredients for a Healthy Life: Very Tasty Vegetable Recipes*. All new material in this edition is authored by Rose Miles.

Cataloging-in-Publication Data
Names: Miles, Rose.
Title: Cooking with veggies / Rose Miles.
Description: Buffalo, NY : Enslow Publishing, 2027. | Series: Kid chefs | Includes glossary and index.
Identifiers: ISBN 9781978548633 (pbk.) | ISBN 9781978548640 (library bound) | ISBN 9781978548657 (ebook)
Subjects: LCSH: Cooking (Vegetables)--Juvenile literature. | Vegetables--Juvenile literature.
Classification: LCC TX801.M674 2027 | DDC 641.5636--dc23

Printed in China

Photos Credits: Cover, p. 1 Peter Hermes Furian/Shutterstock.com; cover, p. 1 New Africa/Shutterstock.com; cover, p. 1 Riccio da favola/Shutterstock.com; cover, p. 1 Mike_O/Shutterstock.com; cover, p. 1 LN team/Shutterstock.com; p. 4, 6, 8, 10, 12, 14, 16, 18, 20 ricorico/Shutterstock.com; p. 5 Art_Photo/Shutterstock.com; p. 7 Almahira hafshah/Shutterstock.com; p. 8 domnitsky/Shutterstock.com; p. 9 Billion Photos/Shutterstock.com; p. 10 DUSAN ZIDAR/Shutterstock.com; p. 11 Erhan Inga/Shutterstock.com; p. 12 mario95/Shutterstock.com; p. 14 OSINSKIH AGENCY/Shutterstock.com; p. 15 Jacek Chabraszewski/Shutterstock.com; p. 16 Pavel Vatsura/Shutterstock.com; p. 17 NataliaZa/Shutterstock.com; p. 19 Pixel-Shot/Shutterstock.com; p. 20 JMP_Traveler/Shutterstock.com; p. 21 zcw/Shutterstock.com

CPSIA compliance information: Batch #QSENS27: For further information, contact Enslow Publishing,
New York, New York, at 1-800-398-2504.

Contents

Recipes in this book may use knives, mixers, and hot stove tops. Ask for an adult's help when using these tools.

Words in the glossary appear in **bold** type the first time they are used in the text.

A World of Color

From the deep red of beets to the bright green of zucchini, vegetables come in all the colors of the rainbow! The flavors and **textures** change from vegetable to vegetable too. Green beans are sweet and crisp, while greens like kale can be chewy and a little bitter.

Lucky for us, all vegetables have lots of **nutrients**, so you can probably eat them as often as you want! Aim to fill half your plate with veggies at dinnertime and eat a vegetable or fruit with every snack and meal.

Do You Have Allergies?

The **recipes** in this book may use **ingredients** that contain or have come into contact with nuts, gluten, dairy products, and other common causes of **allergies**. If you have any food allergies, please ask a parent or teacher for help when cooking and tasting!

It's fun to try new vegetables! Eating many different kinds of veggies gives you the most health benefits. They provide lots of nutrients that your body needs and are important for a healthy ***diet****.*

What Are Vegetables?

Vegetables are the parts of plants that people can eat. Vegetables are often put into one of five groups based on the part of the plant that you eat.

Garlic and onions are bulb vegetables. These are plants that grow below the ground and make bulbs you can eat. Broccoli, cauliflower, and artichokes are flower vegetables because the part of the plant that you eat is the flower. Cabbage, celery, lettuce, and spinach are leaf vegetables because—you guessed it!—you eat the leaves. Root vegetables consist of beets, carrots, radishes, and turnips. And finally, asparagus and kohlrabi are stem vegetables.

Tasty Tidbits

Some foods you may call vegetables are actually fruits, like eggplant, tomatoes, cucumbers, and squash. They're thought of as vegetables because they're more often a dinner food than a dessert food, like strawberries might be.

There are many different kinds of vegetables. Some people say there may be as many as 50,000!

From the Farm to You

When you walk into a grocery store, you might see rows and rows of fresh vegetables. But how did they get there? These vegetables are commonly grown on big farms. They've often traveled a great distance on refrigerated trucks to be placed in your cart and made for dinner.

Other vegetables are **preserved** soon after they're picked. They may be frozen or canned. As long as you choose frozen and canned vegetables that don't have a lot of added salt or creamy sauces, they're still a great choice. Frozen veggies are just as healthy as fresh ones.

Tasty Tidbits

Pickles are made from cucumbers, but other veggies can be pickled too. They're preserved by soaking in a salty liquid called brine for several weeks.

Easy Veggie Soup

makes 4 servings

Ingredients:

1 tablespoon olive oil
1 onion
2 large carrots
1 stalk celery
1 cup green beans
1 zucchini

½ teaspoon salt
¼ teaspoon black pepper
¼ teaspoon oregano
2 cups chicken or vegetable stock
2 tablespoons tomato paste

Directions:

1. Chop the onion, carrots, celery, green beans, and zucchini, and put them into separate bowls.
2. Heat the olive oil in the bottom of a large pot on medium-low heat. Add the onion and stir for about 1 minute.
3. Add the chopped carrot and celery, and season with the salt, pepper, and oregano. Cook for about 3 minutes, stirring a few times.
4. Stir in the chopped zucchini and green beans. Cook together for about 1 minute.
5. Pour in the chicken or vegetable stock, and mix in the tomato paste. Bring it to a boil.
6. Lower thc heat so the soup simmers for about 20 minutes, stirring a few times.

For this veggie soup, use whatever vegetables you have on hand. You could add frozen peas, canned tomatoes, or even spinach. Adding a can of black beans makes this an even healthier, heartier meal.

Eat Your Veggies

There are many ways to prepare vegetables. The key to getting enough veggies in your diet is finding ways you like to eat them!

Root vegetables taste great when they're roasted in the oven. Broccoli and sugar snap peas are delicious stir-fried or eaten raw with dip, such as hummus. You can even chop vegetables like carrots up really small and add them to meatloaf or macaroni and cheese. You're still getting important nutrients your body needs, even if you can't taste it!

Tasty Tidbits

A big, fresh salad is one easy way to get a few servings of veggies. Start with a bed of spinach or chopped romaine lettuce, and then add whatever veggies you have at home. Top with some shredded cheese, sunflower seeds, or avocado. Be creative, and use what you like!

Cinnamon Sweet Potato Fries

makes 4 servings

Ingredients:

2 medium sweet potatoes, cut into ½-inch wedges
3 tablespoons olive oil
1 teaspoon salt
½ tablespoon cinnamon

Directions:

1. Preheat oven to 350 degrees.
2. Put cut sweet potatoes in a big bowl. Pour olive oil over them and toss to coat.
3. Sprinkle the salt and cinnamon over the sweet potatoes. Toss again to get some on all the pieces.
4. Spray a cookie sheet with cooking spray. Spread the sweet potato wedges on the sheet in a single layer. You may need more than one cookie sheet.
5. Bake in the oven for 15 minutes. Turn the sweet potatoes over and return to the oven to bake for another 20 minutes.
6. Serve with ketchup, honey, or peanut butter for dipping!

Sweet potatoes are high in fiber and vitamin A, but they can be hard to cut. Ask an adult for help. Then, enjoy a healthy version of this popular side dish with your next meal!

Time to Eat!

Vegetables contain nutrients called vitamins and minerals. These are important to your body's function and growth. Diets that include lots of vegetables and fruit have been shown to help lower blood pressure and keep your heart healthy.

All vegetables are good for you, but they are good in different ways. Different vegetables offer different nutrients. That's why it's smart—and tasty—to eat lots of different kinds. Plus, you never know when you might find your new favorite!

kale

Tasty Tidbits

Many vegetables, like broccoli, sweet potatoes, and kale, are considered **superfoods**. They're packed with nutrients that help keep you healthy and feeling great.

Vegetables are packed with many health benefits. Check out this list of nutrients your body needs and the veggies that provide them!

NUTRIENT	WHAT IT DOES	WHAT TO EAT
vitamin A	keeps eyes healthy; supports the function of the heart, lungs, and other organs	sweet potatoes, spinach, carrots, summer squash
vitamin C	helps the body fight off illness and grow and repair	peppers, broccoli, Brussels sprouts, kale, potatoes
calcium	builds healthy bones and teeth	celery, cabbage, spring onions, spinach
iron	makes up a part of blood that moves oxygen throughout the body	cooked spinach, Swiss chard, artichokes, beets
potassium	supports **cell**, muscle, and **nerve** health	tomatoes, cucumbers, eggplants, zucchini, pumpkins, potatoes

Spice It Up

Some peppers are hot. Some are not. But no matter what kind of pepper you eat, they're all good for you. Peppers have lots of vitamins A, C, and K. They're great for your eyes and bones and provide lots of **antioxidants**. These nutrients may lessen the risk of heart disease, eye problems, and **cancer**.

If you like spicy food, you're probably familiar with Tabasco sauce. But did you know that Tabasco is a kind of pepper? Along with cherry and cayenne peppers, Tabasco peppers are hot! Sweet peppers, or bell peppers, aren't hot at all. They're tasty sliced and added to stir-fries or eaten raw alongside other crisp vegetables, such as carrots and celery sticks.

Tasty Tidbits

Peppers are native to the Americas. They spread throughout Europe after 1493 when pepper seeds were taken to Spain.

Veggie-Filled Frittata

Makes 6 servings

Ingredients:

1 tablespoon olive oil
4 large eggs
2 cups of tightly packed fresh spinach, chopped
1 cup shredded cheddar cheese
¼ cup red pepper, chopped
3 green onions, sliced
¼ cup fresh tomato, diced
pinch of salt and pepper
fresh basil, chopped

Directions:

1. Preheat oven to 350 degrees.
2. In a pan on the stove top, heat the olive oil on medium heat. Add the pepper and onions. Cook for about 3 minutes, stirring a few times.
3. Transfer the pepper and onions to a bowl. Allow to cool.
4. In another bowl, use a fork or whisk to beat the eggs.
5. Add the cheese, spinach, tomatoes, beaten eggs, salt, and pepper to the cooked pepper and onions. Mix together.
6. Spray a pie plate with cooking spray. Pour the egg mixture into the pie plate.
7. Bake for about 40 minutes, or until a knife inserted in the center comes out clean. Serve slices with chopped basil on top.

A frittata is an egg dish that can be made in lots of different ways. Try different combinations of cheese and vegetables to find your favorite. You can even add some Tabasco sauce on top for an extra kick!

Better Broccoli

Broccoli is a nutrient powerhouse! It's considered one of the healthiest vegetables. It's full of antioxidants and, like many fruits and vegetables, it is a good source of fiber. Fiber is a nutrient that helps move food through your body and out as waste. It also keeps you feeling fuller, which is why vegetables help maintain a healthy weight.

A little cooking brings out a sweet flavor in broccoli. Cut it up into bite-sized pieces and toss with olive oil and salt. Then, bake the broccoli in the oven on a cookie sheet for about 10 minutes. Enjoy that crisp, salty flavor as a healthy snack or side dish!

Tasty Tidbits

Broccoli looks like little trees! People have been eating broccoli since the days of ancient Rome.

Broccoli Stir-Fry

Ingredients:

⅓ cup creamy natural peanut butter
½ cup water
2 tablespoons brown sugar
2 tablespoons reduced-sodium soy sauce
1 tablespoon rice vinegar
2 tablespoons canola oil
1 ½ pounds broccoli crowns, trimmed and cut into 1-inch pieces
1 large red bell pepper, sliced
2 cloves garlic, minced
crushed red pepper flakes
¼ cup chopped unsalted peanuts

Directions:

1. Mix together the peanut butter, ¼ cup water, brown sugar, vinegar, and 1 tablespoon of soy sauce in a bowl and set aside.
2. Heat oil in a large frying pan or **wok** on medium heat. Add the broccoli and allow to cook for about 5 minutes, stirring a few times.
3. Pour in the rest of the water and 1 tablespoon of soy sauce. Stir in the bell pepper and garlic, and cook with the broccoli for about 2 to 4 minutes, or until the water is gone.
4. Turn off the heat. Pour the peanut sauce over the broccoli and pepper and stir well.
5. Serve with a sprinkle of the chopped peanuts and crushed red pepper to each person's taste.

Broccoli is packed with calcium, iron, and lots of other things that are great for your body. Try this tasty broccoli recipe and take in a good dose of this superfood!

Perfect Pumpkin

Pumpkin is popular, especially in the fall. You might see pumpkin-flavored donuts or pumpkin-flavored hot drinks. And of course, Thanksgiving wouldn't be the same without pumpkin pie! But pumpkin can be used for more than just desserts. It is a common—and healthy!—ingredient in chili and sauces.

There are lots of ways to enjoy the taste and health benefits of this yummy vegetable. Try mixing this vitamin C-rich food into vanilla yogurt with a sprinkle of cinnamon. Or take in your daily vitamin A by topping a bowl of oatmeal with pumpkin.

Tasty Tidbits

Pumpkin is often sold as canned **puree** (pyuh-RAY). A great way to include more veggies in your diet is to mix purees into sauces, scrambled eggs, and baked goods. They add flavor and extra nutrients!

Pumpkin Muffins

makes about 30 minimuffins

Ingredients:

1 ½ cups white whole-wheat flour
¾ cup sugar
1 teaspoon baking powder
1 teaspoon baking soda
pinch of salt
1 teaspoon pumpkin pie spice
1 can 100-percent pure pumpkin
2 eggs
½ cup canola oil or vegetable oil
⅓ cup low-fat Greek yogurt

These muffins provide a healthy boost to your breakfast. Besides the pumpkin in them, the whole-wheat flour and Greek yogurt will keep you full until lunchtime!

Directions:

1. Preheat oven to 400 degrees.
2. Spray minimuffin tins with cooking spray.
3. Mix together the flour, sugar, baking powder, baking soda, pumpkin pie spice, and salt.
4. In a separate bowl, combine the pumpkin, eggs, oil, and yogurt.
5. Add the pumpkin mixture to the dry ingredients. Mix well.
6. Use a spoon to fill the muffin tins with batter.
7. Bake for 8 to 10 minutes, or until a toothpick inserted in the middle of one of the muffins comes out clean. Allow them to cool.

Growing a Garden

There's nothing like eating foods you've grown yourself. That sense of pride you feel from picking a juicy, red tomato right off the vine will make it taste even better. Plus, planting your own vegetable garden is a fun way to help your family include even more veggies in their diet!

For beginning gardeners, good foods to grow include carrots, peas, peppers, spinach, and tomatoes. You can make the garden as big as you'd like, or start small with just a tomato plant on your porch. You might just be a future farmer!

Tasty Tidbits

If you don't have a green thumb, you can still eat local vegetables by visiting a farmer's market in your town. These vegetables are often fresher than the ones in your grocery store because they don't have to travel as far.

Why Eat Vegetables?

Vegetables Provide Nutrients

- Potassium keeps nerves functioning properly. The vitamin A in many veggies helps maintain eye health. And so many more!

Vegetables Keep You Healthy

- Diets high in vegetables lessen the risk of heart disease. Antioxidants stop cell damage, aid in repair, and cut cancer risk.

Vegetables Fill You Up

- Many vegetables are full of fiber! That keeps your digestive system working well. And because fiber makes us feel full, eating veggies can stop us from eating too much junk food.

Vegetables are Hydrating

- Many vegetables, like cucumbers, lettuce, and celery, contain a lot of water. Drinking enough water is super important for doing well in sports, thinking clearly, and staying healthy.

Glossary

allergy: a body's sensitivity to usually harmless things in the surroundings, such as dust, pollen, or mold

antioxidants: special molecules that help protect our bodies from harmful things; they keep our cells healthy

cancer: a disease caused by the uncontrolled growth of cells in the body

cell: the smallest basic part of a living thing

diet: the food one usually eats

ingredient: a food that is mixed with other foods

nerve: a part of the body that sends messages to the brain and allows us to feel things

nutrient: something a living thing needs to grow and stay alive

preserve: to keep something in an unspoiled state

puree: the paste or liquid created by grinding or blending cooked food

recipe: an explanation of how to make food

superfoods: foods that are super healthy because they are rich in antioxidants, vitamins, and minerals

texture: the structure, feel, and appearance of something

wok: a large, thin metal pan with a curved bottom

Fact Check

1. What vegetable is a great source of vitamin A?
   a. sweet potatoes
   b. cabbage
   c. beets

2. Cooking brings out a __________ flavor in broccoli.
   a. bitter
   b. sour
   c. sweet

3. Vegetables can be preserved by soaking in a salty liquid called ________.
   a. pickles
   b. brine
   c. puree

Answers: 1. a, 2. c, 3. b

On the Internet

Recipes
www.superhealthykids.com/healthy-kids-recipes.php
Check out this list of healthy, yummy recipes for all your meals!

Vegetables
www.freshforkids.com.au/vegetables/
Find out lots of information about many different kinds of vegetables!

Publisher's note to educators and parents: Our editors have carefully reviewed these websites to ensure that they are suitable for students. Many websites change frequently, however, and we cannot guarantee that a site's future contents will continue to meet our high standards of quality and educational value. Be advised that students should be closely supervised whenever they access the Internet.

Index